No Need To Google God

No Need To Google God

He Is Everywhere

RENAY A. FOSTER

No Need To Google God

He is Everywhere

Renay A Foster

A publication of The Publisher's Notebook Ltd.

NO NEED TO GOOGLE GOD

©2016. Renay A. Foster. All rights reserved.

No part of this book may be reproduced or transmitted in any form or by any means without written permission from the author.

Google™ is a registered trademark of Google Inc.

ISBN: 978-976-95940-5-0

Published by: The Publisher's Notebook Ltd

Email: publisher@thepublishersnotebook.com

Dedication

This book is dedicated to the memory of my biological father, the late, great, Presiding Elder Vernal Spencer who taught me at a very early age to be sensitive to the voice and move of God.

I thank him for the quality time that we spent together, the many times that we passed enjoying nature and revelling in the finery of God's handy work. I am grateful to him for the lessons in cherishing the 'now'. I have learnt and appreciated much especially as I listened to the tributes at his funeral. His life impressed upon me that God is present in everything that we do; whether you help an elderly person cross the street, wipe a child's nose or feed a wild bird.

I thank him for the invaluable life lessons and pray that I will impact generations in a manner comparable to what he did.

To my beautiful mother Jeanette Laurel Spencer whose vigour challenges me to survey the splendour of this earth. As I grow older I am reminded of wealth of wisdom that lingers at her feet.

Table of Contents

Foreword	i
Acknowledgements	ii
Introduction	iv
Goats Don't Have Beaks – Birds Do	1
Removing The Creases	3
Keep Charged!	5
Ripe And Ready	7
Barriers Are Lifted	9
It's Already Done	12
Living Water	15
Child Like Faith	17
Bug Off	19
Temperature Check	24
Order My Steps	27
Time For Turbulence	30
Swarmed By Dogs	33
Blind As A Bat	38
Stripped	40
A Tree Planted	42
Blocked Signal	45
Raising Agent	47
Junior At The Fish Market	49
Get The Vet	51

Up From The Root	53
Because She Cried I Tried	57
We Need The Light	59
Who Could It Be But Jesus?	61
Bite Him	63
About The Author	65

Foreword

In a time with so many distractions it's great to know author Rev Renay Foster has come up with a simple yet profound work of art to refocus readers to connect with God, grow their faith and embrace God's peace knowing that He is in charge.

The analogies are scintillating, riveting and create images in your mind that will cause the lessons to stick like glue!

At the end of this brief read you will end up valuing your uniqueness and trusting God in a great way. It will deepen your walk with God and release a peace that is so invaluable in these times of turmoil. It will cause you to slow down and observe because God is speaking.

No Need To Google God is prophetic, it made me wish I knew her dad. It will help you to discover you. This book will help with your security in God who has full control over all things. It is extremely powerful and deep yet simple. Renay was very thoughtful and careful in her analogies, the illustrations are powerful and will certainly strengthen and deepen your faith. The book is not religious but biblically sound! There are splashes of humour all over this quick read. It will bless you considerably.

Bishop C. McLean

Founder & Pastor Worship And Faith International Fellowship (WAFIF)

Website: http://wafifglory.com

Acknowledgements

My greatest gratitude is to the Lord our God who orders my steps and speaks to me audibly thus enabling me to pen this book. It is true that you understand 'further along.'

I thank God for my wonderful, loving husband Locksley Foster who offers relentless support in all my exploits. I thank him for the days and nights of holding the fort thus allowing me to make this book a reality. His unspoken support overwhelms my heart .

I thank.......

- My mother Jeanette Spencer who is selfless in sharing the experiences that we share.

- Jermaine Spencer, Claudia Spencer-Gordon, Shauna Spencer, Grace Ann Wood and Gabrielle Gordon with whom I interact daily , I thank you for the laughter, the sobering talks and the genuine display of love.

- Bishop, Courtney McLean and my family at WAFIF for creating a good breeding ground for success and an environment conducive to growth.

- Prophet Mark McLean who continues to speak the promises of God concerning my life in my sometimes doubtful ears.

- Stacy Ann Christian my dear friend who has been outrageously selfless in every undertaking.

- Our employees at The Laundry Centre who perform optimally even in my absence thereby allowing the realisation of this dream.

- Nastassia Robinson who conducted the earliest edit, your keen attention to details is invaluable.
- My friends near and far who encourage my feat and assist in making my journey undemanding.

Malachi

Introduction

God asked Jeremiah in Jeremiah 1:11 and 13 "What seest thou? Further in the said chapter, we understand the meaning of what Jeremiah saw. It was a seething pot; with the face toward the north.

There is always a message in what we see and what surrounds us, but we are often too busy to see or hear.

This book will demonstrate how God speaks to us every day in simple ways. It was written with the intent to provoke your awareness and inspire you to see God in everything that you do.

The short stories are very easy to read, they can be absorbed on a short commute to work or while you have a quick bite. It further demonstrates that God is not complicated; it expresses the love of God and His desire to bless, protect and profess His love for us.

The notes at the end will encourage reflection and introspection and challenge you to a level of intimacy that you will unquestionably progressively crave.

Goats Don't Have Beaks – Birds Do

Have you ever noticed how animals are able to fend for themselves when it is time to find food? I further appreciated this by watching some birds who would visit my yard daily in search of food.

A flock of beautiful birds would always gather in my yard under a mango tree to enjoy the pickings. I noticed their habit and decided to give God a hand in providing for these wondrous creatures of the air. I would often throw rice grains for them to enjoy and even provided a pan with water as the days can be very hot.

One day as I sat on my patio, I noticed some goat kids walking through the gaps in my wrought ironed gate. They headed towards the mango tree where I had laid out the feast for the birds and proceeded to drink some of the water. One of kids noticed the scattered rice grains; he went to sniff them out and to further inspect what the grains were. The other kids also joined him in the testing of the goods.

By now, they were trying to pick the grains up with their mouths. After several unsuccessful attempts to pick at and consume the grains, the little goats trotted off seemingly disappointed as their mouths couldn't pick up the grains. They couldn't consume the grains because rice grains are tiny. It was never intended for goats to be able to consume rice grains.

Today, I prophesy to you that whosoever would attempt to devourer what is yours will not be able to do so. I declare that they will be unsuccessful in their exploits. Weapons might form but they will not prosper in Jesus' name

Birds were made with beaks that can pick up the grains but the biological makeup of goats doesn't allow them to do the same. It is the same with you – your enemies cannot occupy or consume what was intended for you. The Egyptians were not able to cross the Red Sea, it was a means of escape for the Israelites. God made you special. There is no other who is just like you. You were fearfully and wonderfully made.

Psalms 139:13-14 *For you created my inmost being; you knit me together in my mother's womb. I praise you because I am fearfully and wonderfully made.*

Malachi 3:11 *And I will rebuke the devourer for your sakes, and he shall be a delightsome land, saith the Lord of Hosts*

Notes:

Removing The Creases

God whispers anywhere; in interesting places, when you least expect it and my place of business also happened to be one such interesting place;

I believe I was born to be an entrepreneur. I explored a number of business ventures before settling into commercial dry and wet cleaning. We own and operate a commercial laundry; it was while I was at work that God chose to whisper to me.

Part of our specialty at the company is steam pressing which requires specialized equipment such as the boiler. The boiler is a piece of equipment that heats water to produce steam which is then used to operate the dryers, washers and press machines. Whenever the steam is released into the pipes, it makes crackling sounds and the black iron pipes are hot to touch. This type of energy is required daily for the operation of the company. The pipes that carry the steam come under intense pressure.

Only after the steam is released can the pressers warm up to carry out their functions. Only with the heat can the washers wash at high enough temperatures to remove stains and bacteria from soiled linen and only by the heat can the purpose of purification and removing creases be achieved.

That's how it is when you carry the fire of God within you. There is great discomfort, you crackle a bit, you expand and contract and the pressure builds up. You might feel like there is an overload and that you might crack under all the pressure but you are made for it. Just as strong iron pipes are used in the boiler instead of feeble plastic ones, you too were created for your purpose.

Do you feel like you are being stretched? Is God sending more heat through your pipes than you think you can handle? What do you believe you were created to do? What special attributes, gifts or talents do you possess that make you unique to carry out that job?

Proverbs 3:6 *"In all your ways acknowledge him, and he will make straight your paths."*

Notes:

Keep Charged!

Like most electronic devices, my iPad requires electrical power in order to operate. My practice is to plug it in overnight for it to be fully charged as it takes a long time to do so.

Like any other night, I carefully inserted the USB cable into the charging port of the tablet and then ensured that it was plugged correctly into the wall outlet. To my surprise, when I awoke the next morning I found that although I had left it on the charger all night, the tablet was uncharged. In fact, the device had died completely. I immediately gave it a quick inspection to see what was happening and I found that it was connected and everything seemed to be in place. After taking a closer look, I realized that I had failed to ensure that the USB cable was properly plugged into the wall socket. I failed to make sure that there was a connection between my iPad and its source of power.

As Christians, we are comparable to electronic devices. We need to be recharged in order to properly function in this world. It is imperative to ensure that you are hooked up to the source of power properly. You need to know who the Source is and ensure that all your switches are turned on.

Do you acknowledge God as the Source of your power? Are you properly connected to God? Are there any loose cables that are preventing you from charging? What's your relationship with the Holy Ghost?

John 15:5

"I am the vine; you are the branches. If you remain in me and I in you, you will bear much fruit"

John 3:3

Jesus answered him. "Truly, truly, I say to you, unless one is born again he cannot see the kingdom of God"

Notes

Ripe And Ready

In Jamaica, we test the ripeness of fruits by a habit known as "feeling up" the fruit. This is done by gently squeezing the fruit to see if it is soft enough to be consumed. It is a common practice for me to "feel up' the mangoes on my trees in a bid to determine the ones that were ripe and fit for consumption.

One day, I glanced through my kitchen window, I observed a mango that appeared very "cherry" in appearance. Surely a fruit with such colour must be fit and ready to eat. As I neared the tree in great anticipation to devour the fruit, my eagerness was shattered. The seemingly 'ripe' mango was not at all fit but rather sunburnt thus having the deceptive rosy colour.

Disappointed, I moved a branch that was in my path in an attempt to make my way back to the confines of my kitchen. As I moved the branch, another mango that was green in appearance fell right off and into my hand. It was ripe but didn't demonstrate a change in colour.

Things aren't always as they appear. The red mango got its colour because of its direct exposure to the sun it wasn't at all ready to be reaped and consumed as I so eagerly wanted to do. The one that was in the shade was fully ready but didn't appear that way.

As was the case with the mango, you might not appear ready to the world but God is secretly preparing you. You have been hidden to protect you from predators. Like the leaves, He is shielding and guarding you. You have been prepared for a bigger harvest.

Don't be disheartened if you don't fit into what the world describes as ready. Be not conformed but be transformed. You were not made to look like the others. You were set apart, you were ordained – predestined. Your qualities and abilities are unique. If you are an eagle don't try to look like a chicken.

Romans 12:2

"And be not conformed to this world, but be ye transformed by the renewing of the mind that ye may prove what is good and acceptable......."

Notes:

Barriers Are Lifted

One morning I experienced the nudge and whisper as I approached the toll plaza that allows passage into the city. As I waited in line to pay, I observed that all the lanes had the green arrows, indicating that there is a working attendant with the exception of one lane that reflected the red X, suggesting that it was closed. As I got closer, I noticed that although the X was red, the attendant was still collecting payments and allowing access.

There was one motor car that was almost at the gate but switched over to a longer line seemingly because of his uncertainty as to whether the lane was opened or closed. He was left in the middle of nowhere for a while until someone granted him access. I proceeded to pay the toll at the gate with the Red X and continued on my way ahead of many others.

I seize this moment to remind you that just as access was granted where the Red X was, so is access granted to you today. If God says you can go through then GO THROUGH!!!!!!! Don't doubt. Don't switch lanes. Don't rest in the middle of nowhere. GO THROUGH!!!!!!! He will lift the barriers. With God ALL things are possible!

Do you doubt God on a move that He wants you to make? Are you afraid to get off the boat or cast your nets? List the areas where you believe that you doubted God .

Matthew 19:26

But Jesus beheld them, and said to them, with men this is impossible; but with God all things are possible

Proverbs 3: 5-8

Trust in the Lord with all your heart and lean not on your own understanding. In all your ways acknowledge him and he will make straight your paths. Be not wise in your own eyes; fear the Lord, turn away from evil. It will be healing to your flesh and refreshment to your bones.

Notes:

It's Already Done

I was at the Toll Plaza again on a different occasion when the Holy Ghost ministered to me. Not wanting to endure the daunting traffic of the regular route I decided to brave the traffic of the toll plaza instead. To my displeasure, the lines for payment were excruciatingly long. The hot sun pierced the un-tinted glass and into my skin.

The lane for persons with tags was empty and flowing freely. It took commuters less than 5 seconds to get their bars lifted and access granted. I approached the lane with the required amount in hand because I was unsure of the balance on my tag that would have me a quicker drive through in a fast lane. I was not careful enough to check the balance and feared being denied access so I stayed in line and progressed at turtle pace. I made my way closer to the barrier, paid my charges and went through to the city.

Subsequent to this experience, I sought the number to check my balance and upon doing so I discovered that I had $1310JMD. That was enough to pay my toll fee ten times! I had ten times what I needed but didn't know. I stayed in the long line because I was unsure of my balance but certain of the cash that was in my hand.

God has everything that you need. You only need to trust Him. Check in with Him before you waste your time and your life. We go through life waiting in lines when you're already topped up. Get connected. Call Him; know His number; know His voice. He'll tell you that you have ten times what you need according to his riches in glory. Drive through with confidence, the barrier is already lifted. It was already paid for.

Are you doubting that God will or has provided for you? Write down the times when you doubted God but your worry turned out to be a waste of your energy.

- ❖ _____
- ❖ _____
- ❖ _____
- ❖ _____
- ❖ _____
- ❖ _____
- ❖ _____

Philippians 4: 19

And my God will supply every need according to his riches in glory.

Matthew 6:31-32

Therefore do not be anxious, saying 'What shall we eat?' or 'What shall we drink?' For the Gentiles seek after these things, and your heavenly Father knows that you need them all.

Notes:

Living Water

I love plants. I have them both inside and outside of the house; they're all around. I had three indoor plants inside my living room that I noticed were looking less than healthy. I put them out in the yard for a little sunlight assuming that a little sunlight was what they needed. To my horror, the leaves got scorched and the plant looked worse. They were not made for the outdoors. I pulled them from the yard and placed them on the patio where there was shade. A few days later there were a few new leaves coming up and the plant started to look healthier. After trimming them a bit and watering them as recommended they slowly began to look healthy again.

Sometimes a good thing might not be good for you depending on your situation. Sunlight is generally beneficial to plants as it helps plants to make their food. Some plants need a lot of sunlight to remain healthy while others, such as indoor plants, do not need direct sunlight. My plants did not need direct sunlight. In fact, my housekeeper later admitted that she had forgotten to water them for over a week and suggested the lack of water as the reason for the drooping plants.

What the plants needed was water not direct sunlight. By placing them outside I ended up causing them damage. My outdoor plants were healthy and happy out in the direct sun because they were made for that but the indoor plants suffered because of it.

Know what type you are. Stay in the shade when you need to be. Don't go out in the sun to be scorched when all you need is water. Understand how to discern your times. Increase in sensitivity to the voice of God by spending time in His presence and reading the bible. Many persons want a quick fix today, people are winding up getting counsel from questionable sources. Ensure that you are being fed with the right thing. Discern your needs and seek God continually to guide you.

He is the living water. **Psalms 1**..... *And ye shall be like a tree planted by the rivers of waters.*

What aren't you watering in your life? What are you giving the wrong nourishment? Reflect on your makeup, reflect on your type. Seek the right food.

Child Like Faith

My eight year old niece, Grace Ann, brings me so much joy. She adds flavour to my life through her songs and dances and her mind-blowing conversations. I can truly say she is the life of the party. We spend many hours together doing nothing while still doing everything.

Whenever she spends time at our home, she enjoys jumping in our bed despite being warned about the possible danger. Grace likes fried plantains, I was in the kitchen one day making her favourite when it occurred to me that she was too quiet for far too long.

I headed to the bedroom and as soon as I opened the door Grace leaped from the bed where she had been bouncing right into my arms whilst yelling "catch me". I dropped the contents of my hand and opened my arms to accommodate my buoyant niece. My heart raced with fright but I held onto the prized possession like my life depended on it.

As soon as I was calm enough, I asked her what if I hadn't caught her. She gave me the most confident look and remarked "aunty I knew you wouldn't let me fall. I was sure". I stopped and pondered for a moment about the faith that Grace-Ann has in my frail hands, I marvelled at her confidence in my ability to protect her. I immediately reflected on whether I am trusting God in that childlike manner.

How confident are you that God will catch you if you leap? I dropped the things in my hand and made sure Grace Ann was safe. How much more will a bigger, exceedingly more capable God do for you? Do you trust Him? Would you leap, knowing that He has you?

What are you afraid to release in God's arms?

Jeremiah 17:7

Blessed is the man who trusts in the Lord, whose trust is the Lord

Notes

Bug Off

Every time I go into my garden I am almost always sure to be eaten alive by sand flies but I love my garden so I endure the ordeal. I diligently water and tend to my plants but I have to do so in quite a rush so as to escape the persistent blood suckers. The task became less than enjoyable as I would require aftercare from being massacred by the winged insects. Daily, I would step out apprehensively and scurry along to complete the task.

After months of torture, it dawned on me that I should probably use a repellent before going out into the battlefield. I armed myself with repellent and stepped out with some measure of confidence and even more scantily clad than other times. On this day, I commenced in my usual speedy mode but soon realised that I was not under the usual attack. Minutes lead to over an hour without a nibble, I relaxed and I soon forgot that the bugs even existed.

When you are not covered under the Blood, or wearing the armour of God you are more vulnerable to attacks. You are susceptible to being penetrated by the gnawing of the enemy.

The moment you are armed with the repellent Blood of Jesus Christ no harm can come near you. A thousand shall fall at thy side and ten thousand at thy right hand.

Are you covered under the blood? Are you protected? Are you operating in confidence? Are you enjoying your life the way God intends, or are you hurrying along trying to dodge the attacks? Are you enjoying life or are you enduring life?

Exodus 12:13

And the blood shall be to you a token upon the houses where ye are: and when I see the blood, I will pass over you, and the plague shall not be upon you to destroy you, when I smite Egypt.

Notes

More Moves, Less Announcements

I dabble in a bit of farming. I experimented with carrots and cabbage and was most pleasantly surprised when I saw them bursting through the soil. It was obvious that the cabbage was cabbage as the leaves were folding nicely. The carrots on the other hand just had a green bush-like plant growing on the surface that made me uncertain as to whether there were carrots under the earth or just some weeds growing.

As the weeks went by, I wondered if the carrots were tiny or even orange in colour, I was concerned about their development. One exciting day I went outback to reap some cabbage when I decided to uproot one of the carrots. Doubtfully, my hand emerged with one of the healthiest looking carrots I had seen in a while. It was bright orange in colour and was of a really encouraging size. I harvested all the carrots and had fresh salads and tasty juice for an extended period.

Sometimes what you see on surface isn't reflective of what's really happening underneath! It wasn't the tip of the iceberg that sank the Titanic! What was true was that I watered them daily, planted them in the right situation and ensured they were planted among the right crops.

May your life be like my carrots. May the real meat of the matter surprise you!

Continue to nourish your spirit with the right things! People will doubt who you are but when you are a carrot you don't need to announce it: let your fruit speak! You may appear to be just green bush on the surface but when uprooted, your 'carrot' will be revealed. By your fruit ye shall know them.

Are you feeding your spirit man the right food? Are you among the right crowd? You might appear abnormal or not even bearing fruit, but keep watering, stay away from weeds and your tree will bear the right fruit.

What fruit are you nurturing?

John 15 :1,5

I am the true vine and my father is the gardener. I am the vine, you are the branches.

Notes

Temperature Check

Jaguars are known to be reliable cars but the one I was driving started to overheat very early one morning on my way to work. I pulled over to the soft shoulder and help came in a nip. The engine of the car was allowed to cool and coolant added to the panting beast. I was then escorted to the nearest technician for assessment. Preliminary checks revealed that the thermostat was faulty; the part was sourced and subsequently replaced.

After the repair, I was still apprehensive about driving the car. My eyes were almost constantly set on the temperature gauge and as precaution; I checked and topped up the coolant daily despite being told it was okay. I slowly became more comfortable and increased the intervals at which I checked the level of the coolant but was overly reactive if the car went over a pebble or to the slightest sound I heard.

I soon forgot the thermostat after a month of checking the coolant level every three days. Another week went by and I drove and worshipped in my usual fashion. The air in the car grew hot, my eyes immediately went to the gauge, the warning light was on; the needle was on red! My stomach sank and my knees weakened momentarily but I soon regained my composure and pulled the car over to the soft shoulder. Help came and the procedure was the same with the exception that I insisted on going to the dealer and not the nearest technician. They hooked the car up on a diagnostic machine and it revealed all the faults; there was a hose leak and the water was leaking out slowly. There were physical checks for other possible causes and the hose was repaired and I was on my way. I felt more comfortable driving this time considering that the dealer had examined and repaired the car.

It is the same with God, He is the dealer: He knows everything about you. Don't get a quick fix when you need to be thoroughly examined by the dealer. You might be replacing a thermostat when you really had a hose leak. Hook up with the dealer. Although the dealer was further away and more expensive, I had all confidence driving after their assessment and repair. The car ran smoothly with no complaints except that broken wiper blade but that's another story!

Where do you go when you are overheating? When you are overly exhausted? When you need repair? Are you getting a quick fix in areas of your life that need the dealer? God is the dealer and the Bible is the manual. Do not settle for quick fixes.

Isaiah 45:7

I form light and darkness, I make well-being and create calamity, I am the Lord, who does all these things.

Ephesians 3:9

And to bring to light for everyone what is the plan of the mystery hidden for ages in God who created all things

Order My Steps

I love travelling. I love going to new and interesting places to find the hidden beauty of the world. London swiftly became one of my favorite places as, in addition to being the home of my mother, I love the obvious and ineradicable history visible all around London. As I traversed London, I hopped the trains like a native of the land. The only caution was that I get on the right train. Nobody checked my destination therefore it was entirely up to me, except when my then fiancé (now husband) would meticulously map my route. It didn't matter where I was going as long as I had sufficient funds on my Oyster Card[1] to get me there. I missed my steps a few times but easily corrected my miscalculations and was back on track. A few weeks of Trafalgar Square[2], Buckingham Palace[3], Bullring[4] in Birmingham and posh Pinner and it was time to journey back home.

As I left for Jamaica, the land of my birth, I checked in at Gatwick Airport[5] and arrived home nine hours later. As

---

[1] A *Visitor Oyster Card is a quick and easy way to pay for travel on public transport in London.*

[2] *Trafalgar Square is a public space and tourist attraction in central London, built around the area formerly known on the Oyster card as Charing Cross.*

[3] *Buckingham Palace is the London residence and principal workplace of the reigning monarch of the United Kingdom.*

[4] *Shopping and leisure complex.*

[5] *Airport in London.*

I waited briefly at immigration, I realized the differences between hopping trains and catching a plane. I realized that for the airplane I needed a ticket to a named destination: money on a card wasn't enough. I also needed a valid passport/identification. This time around, someone checked where I was going; it wasn't up to me to get off at a point, the pilot headed directly to the destination.

On the train, I was prone to get off at the wrong stop. I could hop the wrong train sometimes I wasted valuable time and ended up right where I started out. On the plane however, I had to go through security checks, I couldn't get off anywhere but my stop. The pilot was in control.

Let God be your pilot. He'll get you there safely. Book your ticket and let Him teach you things along the way. Confess that He's Lord and get onboard.

Do you trust God to be your pilot? Are you hopping trains or taking the plane?

Proverbs 16:9

A man's heart plans his ways, but the Lord directs his steps

Notes:

Time For Turbulence

I like British Airways. However, the skilled pilots and the well-built aircrafts couldn't prevent the turbulence that we would experience en route to London. We took off and ascended smoothly. Meals were served, movies watched, books read, babies slept and grown folks snored. My club world seat was fully converted to a bed and sleeping was easy but I was awakened by extreme vibrations onboard.

The aircraft shuddered, the fasten seatbelt sign was illuminated, passengers were alert and looked scared, flight crew had no expression on their faces and the pilot was quiet.

We grew closer to our destination, the purser announced that we were approaching and advised us to prepare accordingly and we started our descent. The Holy Spirit started to speak…..

The turbulence we experienced was when we were breaking the clouds and nearing our destination. The pilot had by now apologized for the humps and bumps and assured us that they were behind us. He mentioned that the weather was beautiful where we were headed, that he had passed through some bad patches but they were behind us.

Sometimes when you experience turbulence, either God might be taking you through a storm without your knowledge or you are about to land. You might feel uneasy, dizzy, uncomfortable or even scared when you are descending, but descending isn't always a bad thing. It means you are about to arrive at your destination. I noted how quiet the pilot was during the turbulence. He spoke only after we were through the rough spots; that is how it is with God.

He already knows there will be turbulence but He has it under control. He sits at the front with all control buttons under his grasp. Although we may panic and experience discomfort, He knows where we need to go. He already mapped and knows the route, He might not speak while you panic but trust Him.

Is there any turbulence in your life? Do you doubt the capability of your pilot and His crew? Do you know who your captain is?

Remember it's a journey not a destination you might have to take off again. Be prepared. You might experience more turbulence. Fasten your seatbelt.

Psalms 32:7-8

Thou art my hiding place, thou shalt preserve me in trouble, thou shalt compass me about with songs of deliverance. I will instruct thee and teach thee in the way which thou shalt go: I will guide thee with mine eye.

He won't hit you in the spot that you have covered. He won't hit you in the area of your strength where you are guarded.

Notes:

Swarmed By Dogs

My beloved related to me that as a youngster, he loved to 'lock the streets'. It was customary for him to be the last person to come home. In deep rural Jamaica there wasn't much to do for entertainment apart from the occasional wake, concert or church crusade. With very little to do at nights, street lights far and few between, Locksley would often wander a little further than his gate to catch some action.

As he returned home - streets dark, no cars in sight - the only faint light being that of a little shop where adult folks would gamble the night away around a table with one lamp above their heads. One night as he neared the shop, a wolf like pack of dogs encircled him and launched their attack. Standing seemingly hopeless in the middle, the dogs behind him would take bites at him while the ones in front barked and pushed him back into the mouths of the rear guards. His Achilles' were now weakened so he decided to make a run for it. Locksley recalled with a grin how he started kicking at the dogs facing him whilst ignoring the nips at the back. He managed to jump over the pack and run to rescue into the nearby shop.

As he left the shop to continue his journey, he armed himself with as many stones as he could humanly manage. His Samsonite strength paid off but it was his David-like ability that got him home safely after wounding a few with his stones. Without a catapult he conquered his little giants that night. He was undeterred by that occurrence but on subsequent late night trips he would load up with arms and ammunition before approaching the enemy's camp. He would announce his arrival to his enemies by knocking the stones together. Like Pavlov's dogs they remembered how they were previously wounded and would bark from a distance.

Isn't it just like the enemy to lay wait for your soul in the dark? Isn't it just like them to encircle you, distract you and attack your from behind? If you know your enemy, arm yourself with the word of God and sound them when you approach their camp they will stay afar. Let the word of God be continually in your mouth. When the opposition mounts the Spirit of the living God will raise up a standard. He will fight those who fight you. He said so in Psalms 35. They'll remember their blows and wounds. Arm yourself with the word of God. He will give His angels charge over thee. He will protect your going out and your coming in.

Are you armed? The bible is your sword; do you know how to use it?

Psalms 91:4-5

He will cover you with his wings, you will be safe in his care; his faithfulness will protect and defend you. You need not fear any dangers at night or sudden attacks during the day or the plagues that strike in the dark or the evils that kill in daylight.

Notes:

Ant Attitude

There were ants everywhere. They created their own tracks. They ate everything. They were especially in my kitchen. I had a jar of sugar on my counter; it was under heavy siege. I placed it in water to prevent them climbing up the jar, they found a way. If there was fruit nectar for a minute they would find it. If I wiped it with cloth, they would swarm the cloth. I sprayed them, I poisoned them but they were all-pervading. I resorted to placing everything in the refrigerator as they didn't quite seem to like the temperature in there.

I observed a few things about the ants: they were very determined. They travelled in a line in unison on a particular path. If I wiped a few of the ants out, the others didn't stop. If I sprayed their track, they would re-form another track almost parallel to the original one. They bit me viciously whenever I tried to stop them.

As Christians today, are we as determined? Are we as united? They lack in physical strength, but united they hoisted and carried a chicken bone which is many times their body size. When they were attacked and sent off track they found a way, are we that persistent in spreading the gospel? If we're prevented from preaching on buses do we use our status messages to preach? If we are told to turn the church music down do we still sing softly or do we stop?

Let's take on the attitude of the ants. How can you be more like the ants in your walk with God and your daily obligations?

Philippians 4: 13

I can do all things through Christ which strengtheneth me.

Ruth 1 16-18.

And Ruth said ' Intreat me not to leave thee, to return from following after thee: for whither thou goest I will go; and where thou lodgest I will lodge: thy people my people, and thy God my God.

Blind As A Bat

It was 3 am. I flipped the lights on and one of my greatest fears faced me. There it was, flapping its wings in disarray blindly in the light: the bat. Obviously disoriented, it hit every wall, bounced in the fluorescent bulb and finally falling onto the dressing table. I flipped the lights off and he flew towards the door as if he could see. I switched the lights back on and he was back to a state of stupor. I realized that he couldn't function with the lights on. I seized this opportunity to floor my fear with a nearby broom while his mobility was impaired.

God is the light of the world, His light eliminates all darkness. Shine His light on your fears and impair the senses of the adversary. Know what conditions are favorable and favorable to your enemies and use them to your advantage. Your enemies operate in the darkness of anonymity; they will attack when they have the advantage. When you affect their vision, you will impair their mobility.

What areas of your life are in the dark? What is cornering you? How can the light of the Word help defeat your fears?

Psalms 23:4

Even though I walk through the valley of the shadow of death, I will fear no evil, for thou art with me; your rod and your staff, they comfort me.

Notes:

Stripped

I have a severe case of eczema[6]. I make frequent visits to the dermatologist resulting in me having to get a chemical peel along with other creams and dietary restrictions. A special chemical is administered for the peel that stings like a million bees when applied. The chemical removes the layer of dead cells on my skin, leaving my face looking baby young. The stings are almost unbearable but I am always aware of the good that it results in.

A few days after the peel, my skin would start peeling off. At times I appeared two toned, my makeup doesn't match and I don't want to be seen in public for the two week period that it would take to normalize. After the two weeks period, my confidence would be boosted; I would start loving my skin again.

Isn't it just the same when God is stripping us? It hurts initially and might even seem unbearable but it is for the better good. When He's done stripping and peeling you off, you will look better and be healthier. You might be afraid to be in public when you are being stripped.

Is God stripping anything from you? Has He stripped anything from you? How did you feel during the process? How did you feel afterwards?

---

[6] **Eczema**- *A medical condition that cause the skin to become inflamed or irritated.*

2 Corinthians 4:17

Our light affliction, which is but for a moment, is working for us as a far more exceeding and eternal weight of glory.

A Tree Planted

I had two mango trees that produced arguably the sweetest mangoes around town. One of the trees had mangoes in and out of season while the other had mangoes only in season. They were both St. Julian mango trees - same age - so I was baffled as to the reason they were different. We were in the peak of our hurricane season although we had had no direct impact from the storms in the region there were many near misses; consequently, we had excess rainfall from one of the storms.

During this period of heavy downpour, both trees were extremely fruitful and I was amazed at the harvest. The rain soon subsided and shortly after the change in the harvest was obvious.

My investigative mind went in high gear and it dawned on me that the difference now was the absence of the rain. This was made evident when we had three consecutive weeks of heavy rainfall; the same tree had mangoes falling from it in abundance, I didn't have hands to reap them. My neighbours made juice, we made mango chutney with dinner, we had excess of the fruit.

I observed that the tree that bore fruit constantly was close to a pipe the other out in the yard away from the pipe. . It wasn't until then that I figured out that the other tree gave fewer mangoes because it depended on us to water it while the other tree benefitted from the frequent water activities at the pipe. The pipe also had a small leak that I never noticed. It made all the sense in the world.

Psalms 1 tells you that you shall be like a tree planted by the rivers of water that bringeth forth its fruit. People marveled at how this St. Julian mango tree had mangoes even out of its season. I realized that it was the constant supply of water why the harvest was so grand. God is the living water; He is your constant supply. He will keep you supplied and cause you to flourish in and out of your season. When others are not flourishing, He will cause you to thrive.

Are you close to the supply?

Isaiah 55:1

Come all you who are thirsty, come to the waters.

Jeremiah 2:13

For my people have committed two evils; they have forsaken me the fountain of living waters, and hewed them out cisterns, broken cisterns that can hold no water.

Notes:

Blocked Signal

I applied and paid handsomely for cable service at home. After the technicians came in and installed it, the service was second to none. The 'decorator' in me chipped in and I shifted the stand with the cable box and placed it exactly under the wall mounted television. After I shifted around, I was unable to use the remote to carry out its regular functions so the television remained unmoved on TBN.

I started to troubleshoot, I checked the cables lest they had shifted, I changed the remote batteries, I tried every trick.

After a week, I was extremely aggravated and returned the remote to the cable company which was 25 minutes away from my home. Whilst in the shop, they tried the remote and it worked and I felt really silly. I knew something was wrong but I was uncertain as to what it was. A technician asked if I had a flat screen television and if the cable box was close to it, I confirmed that to be true. They subsequently explained that the signal from the television was blocking the signal to the box. On my return home, I moved the cable box from under the television and the remote worked perfectly.

It is also true that if you are under the coverage of the blood of Jesus Christ, the strong signal will block anything that attempts to control you.

What is blocking your signal? Are you under the right coverage? What is preventing your buttons from functioning optimally?

Psalms 91:1

He that dwelleth in the secret place of the most high shall abide under the shadow of the almighty.

Think of the things that Christ has prevented from accessing you. Where would you be had it not been for His grace? Count your blessings, list some.

Notes:

Raising Agent

I learnt a few things at the feet of my knowledgeable mother. It's truly amazing how much you can learn when you really listen to your parents. As I assisted her in baking a cake, my pastry chef of a mother instructed me to keep the butter at room temperature, use a wooden spoon, grate the lemon and break the eggs individually before combining them. A lot of effort went into baking this traditional wedding cake. I looked around and noticed that there many different tools. There was a blender for the breadcrumbs but it was different from the blender for the soaked fruits. There was a grater for the lemon to get the rind but a mixer to cream the butter and sugar. I realized that you couldn't use a blender when you needed a grater. You can't rebuke a devil when you need to forgive someone. Like the butter, you have to be at the right temperature, you can't be cold when you need to be on fire for God. Don't break all your eggs in one bowl; there might be a bad one. Be careful of your associations, deep calls unto deep.

My mind was almost blown away when I reckoned that the ingredients by themselves were not edible although I licked the pan once the batter was ready. The heat from the oven was needed to bake the cake as the raw ingredients couldn't be consumed.

So it is that we need God, without Him as the raising agent and the solidifier, we would all be like raw ingredients.

How do you believe God has processed you? Which areas in your life do you think need some fire?

Notes:

Junior At The Fish Market

At the fish market it is always a hassle. The minute your vehicle pulled up, vendors would rush to try to "get the sale". I felt bad having to choose one vendor and not the other.

After a few trips, I decided to make an arrangement with one of the vendors to have my fish ready by the time I got there. The fish are kept alive until you got there, after purchasing, they would prepare the fish for delivery. I took Junior's number and I would call to place my order complete with describing the truck I drove and all.

As I approached the market, the usual rush was on but Junior remained calm and strutted his stuff as he walked with his head held high and his shoulders squared. He knew that he already had the sale. You could hear him saying "excuse me" as he made his way through the crowd.

Like Junior when you know that your goods are already paid for, the way Christ paid for our sins on Calvary you operate different. There is a intensity of confidence in how you pray and how you approach life. No longer would you be required to rush with the crowd and compete. The anxiety is eliminated from your life as you peruse the bible and understand that your arrangements are already made.

Psalms 46:10

Be still and know that I am God.

Jeremiah 29:11

For I know the plans that I have for you……

Notes:

Get The Vet

We love our dogs, my husband and I searched long and hard to find them. We traversed the pages of the newspaper, trudged the World Wide Web and finally found them in St. Catherine. They are a lovely pair and bring us much joy.

Nine months after they were welcomed in our home, Xena received a bite from her male sibling, Spartacus who probably forgot they were brother and sister. The result of this moment of indiscretion was a very infected wound that had gone unnoticed due to Xena's coat. Upon discovery of the thing we feared the most, we started treating the wound with a spray that we hoped would have helped.

The wound worsened as the days passed and we placed a phone call to their regular vet and he was at our door the very afternoon. He held our precious little Xena and shaved the area and cleaned it. He then administered a cream and gel, unknown to us, and used an instrument to spread the treatment into the wound. Xena railed and kicked and fought but was subdued by her master. She eventually came to a relaxed posture and soon forgot her turmoil. The very next day, we examined the wound and to our shock and amazement, it was significantly improved. Forty eight hours later, Xena was her old self again.

The vet obviously knew what she needed, he was trained and qualified, he cleaned and exposed the area then he treated it. As I reflected on the whole process; I reckoned that it was the same with us and God. Many of us are wounded and try unsuccessfully to treat our selves without success. Our situations worsen as the days go by. Why don't you just call out to our Lord and savior? He will fix it for you; he has the right medication for your wounded soul. He is waiting.

I challenge you today to stop trying to selfheal. He paid the price, he was already wounded for all our transgressions, and He does house calls. Call unto him, he will answer.

Jeremiah 33:3

Call unto me and I will answer thee and shew you great and mighty things which thou knowest not

Notes:

Up From The Root

As a child growing up, I got boils quite frequently. Boils are hardened pimples that had discoloured pus and hurt very badly. I had boils in places that severely restricted my movements. I recall one particular boil on my thigh. I hopped to and fro. Mommy threatened to clean it and get the pus out but I guarded that boil as if my life depended on it. I knew how much it would hurt to have it squeezed for the pus to come out. I would often pretend to squeeze it with the hope that mom wouldn't attempt the feat. I played around with it sometimes placing a band aid on it.

As sure as you guessed it, it festered. I went to sleep one fateful night, and while I slept mom squeezed the boil until the root popped out. I remember alighting from my bed and being airborne for several seconds well past the norm. It was not a pleasant experience. I avoided contact with my mother for a few days.

I noticed however that my limp was significantly improved, the lymph swellings had subsided and it was more tolerable to touch the once out of service zone. A hole was evident but it was now truly healing. I was able to play hop scotch within the day.

I would like to suggest to you that there may be areas of your life that need to be uprooted and properly cleaned. You might be putting a bandaid on a boil that is festering. Why not take it from the root, see what is hurting you or causing you discomfort. When you truly take it to the root, then healing will take place. You will no longer limp through life but you will be able to move unrestricted and uninhibited.

Matthew 16:13

But he answered and said, Every plant, which my heavenly Father hath not planted, shall be rooted up.

Note

Already Provided

I have a terrible practice of not charging my mobile phone. I needed the use of the phone one day but soon realized that it was critically low and I forgot to pack the charger. I was frantic as I received a call about a potential contract and was advised that there would be a follow up call to cement the deal.

I perspired profusely as my husband was now taking another call on the soon to be lifeless phone. I beckoned to him on many occasions expressing deep concern as to the survival of this phone but it totally disregarded my anxious attempt. I grew warmer in the blood as I beckoned to him to use another phone. My effort to get his attention proved futile and I grew warmer. He concluded his call then gently took the charger from his man purse and proceeded to connect same to the distressed phone. I was initially annoyed that he knew he had it and refused to ease my pain but I heard a gentle whisper from the Holy Spirit saying "Your provisions are already made".

So often we pray and cry out to God about things, we get anxious because he is not audible enough. We live our lives like me that day worrying about things that God already has covered even when we are negligent.

Philippians 4:6-7

Do not be anxious about anything, but in everything by prayer and supplication with thanksgiving let your requests be made known to God. And the peace of God, which surpasses all understanding, will guard your hearts and your minds in Christ Jesus.

Notes:

Because She Cried I Tried

We were super excited about our expectant niece or nephew since it had been seven years since we experienced an addition to the family. As each day passed, we grew happier as there had been a spate of mishaps and miscarriages in the bloodline.

Twenty five weeks had passed when we received news that Claudia was admitted in hospital and was positioned to give birth. The doctors were not very hopeful about the survival of the severely premature fetus. The team of doctors proceeded to deliver baby Gabrielle after several medical attempts to delay the birth.

The hour had come on July 13, 2014, Claudia was whisked away to the delivery room to give birth. The unspoken conclusion was that they would preserve the mother's life and just allow the fetus to exit her body. Baby Gabrielle was in a breech position that further complicated matters. The less than two pounds miracle entered the world kicking, as she exited, she gave the loudest cry her underdeveloped lungs could manage. The pediatrician bolted like Usain Bolt with the baby to an incubator and proceeded to administer care.

Upon discourse with the doctor after the ordeal, the doctor stated that she tried because the baby cried, she mentioned that she didn't expect her to be alive.

They were not expecting the baby to survive, especially considering her breeched position.

They further stated the baby would possibly be blind and deaf, would probably have brain defects and would not survive past thirty six (36) hours.

One year and four months later, Gabrielle is attending preschool. She was given a clean bill of health, she had to be placed on a diet to lose weight, and she is speaking a few words and is making attempts to walk.

I know some of you are in a position today that looks dismal, I sense that you have been written off and possibly left for dead. I believe however, that, if like baby Gabrielle, you open your mouth and cry out to the one who stills the water, He will deliver you. I believe that if you push through the odds and play deaf to the naysayers God will show up like he did for baby Gabrielle .

He said in **Jeremiah 33: 3**, *If you call unto him, he will shew you great and mighty things that you know not.*

But I believe that he wants you to call. There are so many accounts in the bible that teach us that some effort is needed on our part. Zaccheus climbed a sycamore tree; the woman with the issue of blood tugged the hem of his garment.

I implore you today to cry out …..The righteous cry, and the LORD heareth, and delivereth them out of all their troubles.

We Need The Light

I love talking with my siblings; we talk several times per day every day. I was having one such daily conversation with Shauna when the light hit me.

Shauna gave a vivid account of an experience that one could have easily overlooked, quite frankly I had forgotten about it.

Our parents were separated in the early nineties; that separation was very stressful for us as children as I'm sure it was for them. Dad was living elsewhere and we sometimes had to traverse three neighbourhoods to catch up with him for lunch money.

One day around dusk, Shauna and I mounted our bikes and headed to visit dad. We had to carefully navigate a bridge because it had a large hole in the middle. We dodged potholes and had quite a laugh along the way as we went on our bike trail. We rode into the evening until it got much darker, there were spots that had street lights but there were many spots that were not well lit. As we rode, we didn't see a high mound of sand that was placed on the side of the road for construction; the lack of light and the dark colour of the hardened sand made it difficult to see the mound. I was a little ahead of Shauna so my wheels hit the mound first, I screamed on the top of my breath "Shauna hold on". The speed at which we were travelling coupled with the hardened state of the sand brought us right over the mound, we were air borne for a while but we landed safely. We laughed hysterically at ourselves but were soon on our way after checking tyres and all.

We eventually made it to dad; the sight of us on our bikes in the night broke his heart but we reassured him that we were fine.

Both our bikes couldn't fit in dad's car so he suggested that we ride and he drove slowly behind us to ensure our safety and also to give light in the dark places. We travelled well and chuckled at the sight of the sand mound that was now well illuminated. We felt so much safer knowing that daddy was behind us plus the lights from the car shone brightly to show us the way.

I want you to know that not every hump or bump is to kill you, they can elevate you.

God is your guide, He is there with you all the way, He lights the way for you. Yea though you walk through the valley of the shadow of death He is with you.

Psalm 32:8

I will instruct thee and teach thee in the way which thou shalt go; I will guide thee with mine eye.

Who Could It Be But Jesus?

It was the year of the dreadful nineteen eighty election in Jamaica. It was a challenging period, there was food shortage, shopkeepers 'married' items, i.e if you wanted to buy soap you would have to buy flour. Financially it was a tough time in the country for families in general.

My parents hit hard times as my dad was working while my mom was a fulltime homemaker. There was heightened violence in the country, the political fervor created unrest in many communities.

The community that we lived in was also faced with challenges. I was around three years old, my sister Claudia was a few months old and my older sister Karlene was eleven. The family had been facing harsh times as the violence also restricted my father's ability to work gainfully. Things got really bad to the point where there was little to no food on the table. The mouths were many that needed to be fed and the money was dwindling by the hour. My parents were never moved by what faced them, the anchored their faiths in the Lord our God. My dad and mom's recollection of the happenings at the time both concurred….they always church and we were always in Sunday school.

Dad told me how our neighbour had raffle tickets for sale from her school and the first prize was cash and the second prize was a basket of groceries.

My parents had long forgotten about purchasing the raffle ticket and were at home carrying out regular chores. It was raining cats and dogs and there was no food in the house. Mommy explained that she heard a faint knock at the gate in the midst of the rain. They wondered if anyone could have braved the downpour, but when dad ran outside he saw the teenage girl holding a box in her hands. Dad ran outside, took the box and showed her to the verandah for shelter. Mom explained how dad stood in the rain holding the box up to heaven with tears streaming down his face giving God thanks.

We won second prize.......God knew that first prize wouldn't have made the impact that second place did. The box contained everything that the family needed with the exception of baby formula.

God knows what you need and he knows when you need it; he knows when the second prize is what you need.

I submit to you today, that if you trust God and obey his instructions, he will see you through. He knows exactly what you need and he is indeed Jehovah Jireh.

Bite Him

Mommy leaned her head as she recalled the encounter when I was but two years old. Mom recounted the incident with precision.......

"You were two years old, I started to teach you about the insects and that some would bite, I called them 'bite him'. Whenever we saw insects, you would shout 'bite him'.

The neighbours loved you; they would often lift you over the fence to spend time with them. One day as you played in the yard next door, I could hear you from our home screaming 'bite him.....bite him....bite him'. When I looked over the fence, I saw you backing up speedily while screaming 'bite him'. There was a frantic cry for help coming from your little body. I couldn't help but leap over the fence to run to your rescue, as I got closer I saw a jet black scorpion with tentacles erect coming at you. I swept you from the ground into my arms and put you in safety then I reached for the scissors and captured and killed the scorpion"

As mom related the story I couldn't help but relate that incident to how we ought to be with God.....there must be a language that we share that He will know your cry. There ought to be a sound that will get His attention.

Mom and I developed our language from spending time together and communicating.

Are you spending enough time with your father? Is there a language that you both share? Does He know the cry of desperation?

God will always protect you, He says He is your shepherd, He said yea though you walk through the valley of the shadow of death, you should fear no evil because He is with you. He also said when the enemy comes in like a flood He will lift up a standard.

I challenge you this day to establish a language that God understands. He understands your tears, He understands moanings and groanings. He is ready to protect you.

Psalm 121

He will not suffer thy foot to be moved: he that keepeth thee will not slumber.

Behold, he that keepeth Israel shall neither slumber nor sleep.

The LORD is thy keeper: the LORD is thy shade upon thy right hand. 6The sun shall not smite thee by day, nor the moon by night.

The LORD shall preserve thee from all evil: he shall preserve thy soul.

The LORD shall preserve thy going out and thy coming in from this time forth, and even for evermore.

About The Author

Ambassador Reverend Renay A Foster is an Entrepreneur, motivational speaker and preacher who connects with persons at all levels by virtue of the journey that life has taken her on. Renay was born in the parish of Kingston, Jamaica. As a pastor's daughter, Renay grew up in the fear of the Lord but wandered from that path in her teenage years. She rekindled the burning fire and surrendered to the call on her life in March, 2012.

This influential woman was ordained as Reverend, Chaplain and Ambassador to The United Nations on August 28, 2015 in the State of New York, she speaks fluent French and currently ministers in North America, Europe and the Caribbean. Renay holds many certificates in various fields but the most important was the one she received at her baptism. She carries a burden to educate abused women especially those who seek love in the wrong places.

Renay is married to Locksley Foster who is her business partner and best friend, they currently reside in St. Catherine , Jamaica.

Contact Information:

Email: Renayamoy1@gmail.com

Telephone: (876) 286-3343

www.ingramcontent.com/pod-product-compliance
Lightning Source LLC
Chambersburg PA
CBHW071408040426
42444CB00009B/2142